AF228660

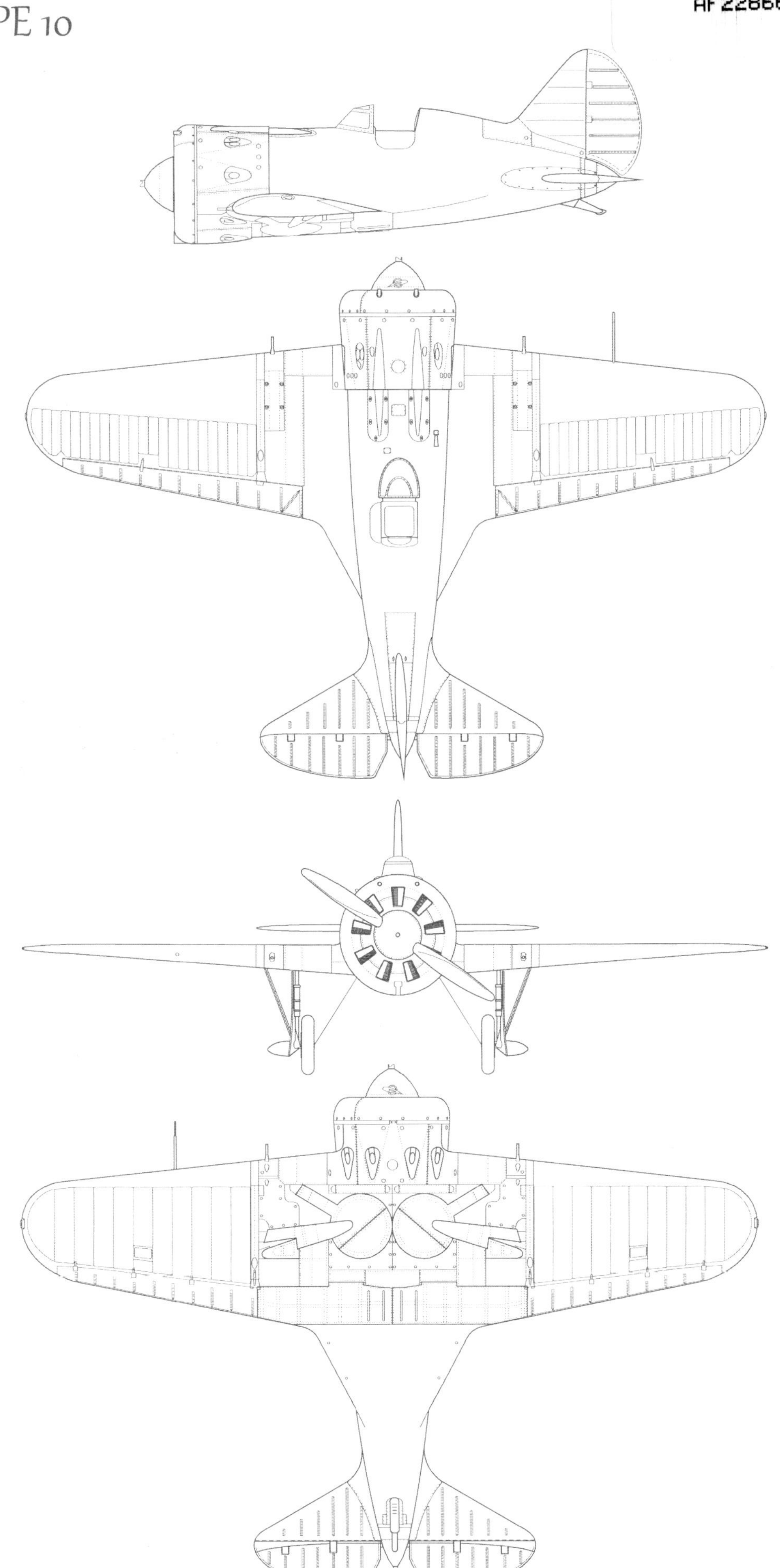

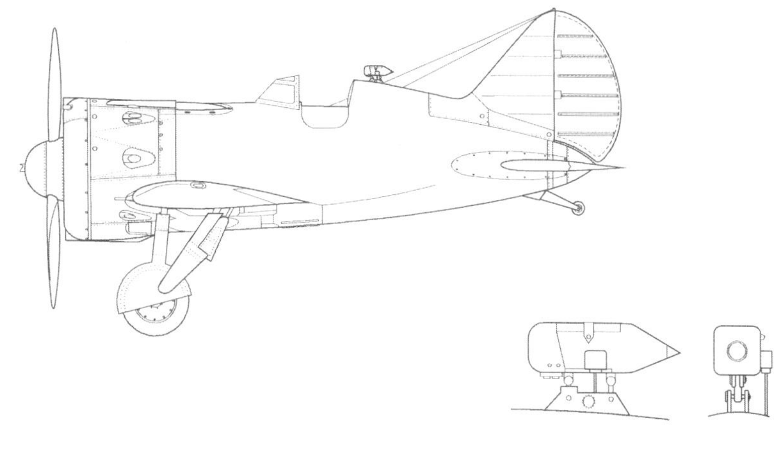

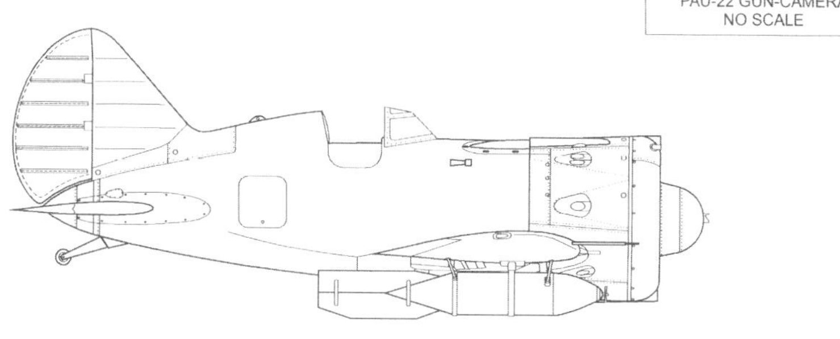
PAU-22 GUN-CAMERA
NO SCALE

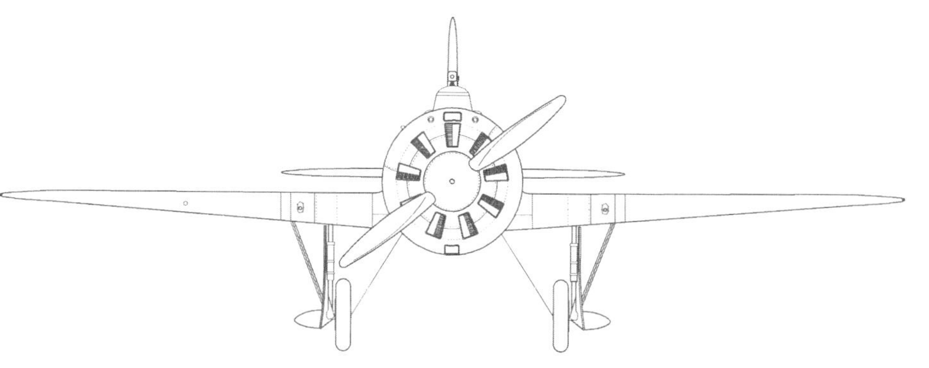

I-16 TYPE 5

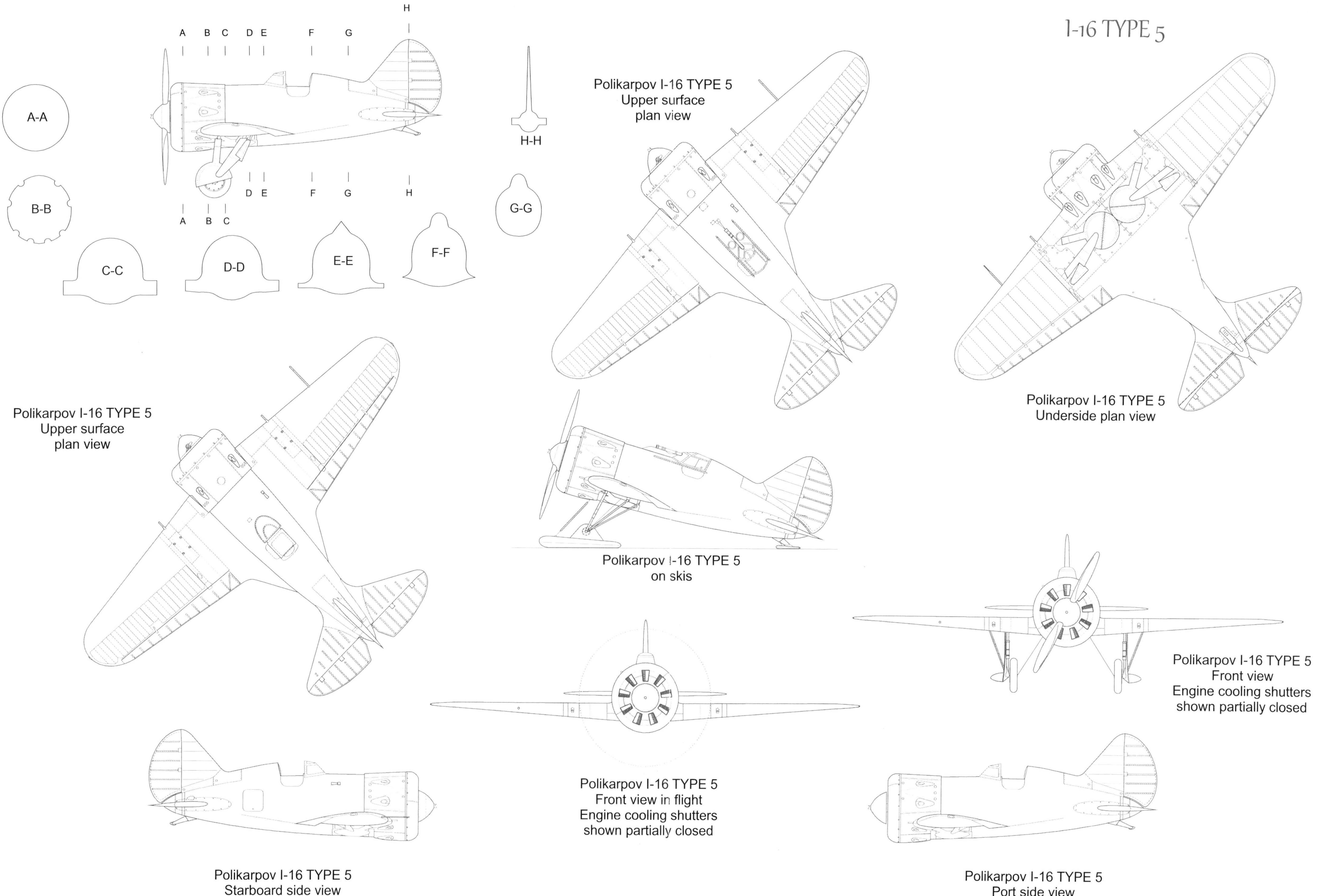

Polikarpov I-16 TYPE 5
Upper surface
plan view

Polikarpov I-16 TYPE 5
Upper surface
plan view

Polikarpov I-16 TYPE 5
Underside plan view

Polikarpov I-16 TYPE 5
on skis

Polikarpov I-16 TYPE 5
Front view
Engine cooling shutters
shown partially closed

Polikarpov I-16 TYPE 5
Front view in flight
Engine cooling shutters
shown partially closed

Polikarpov I-16 TYPE 5
Starboard side view

Polikarpov I-16 TYPE 5
Port side view

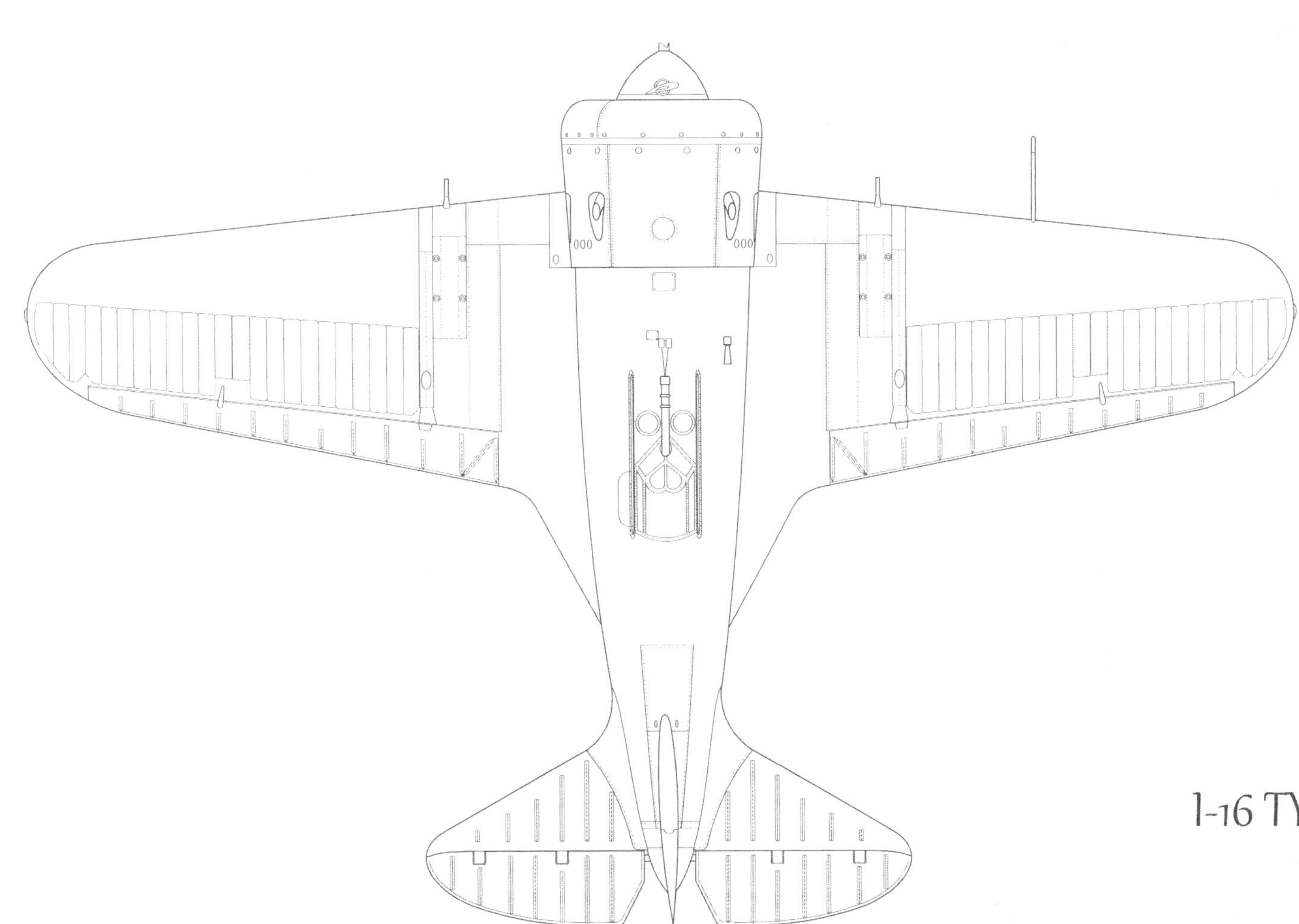

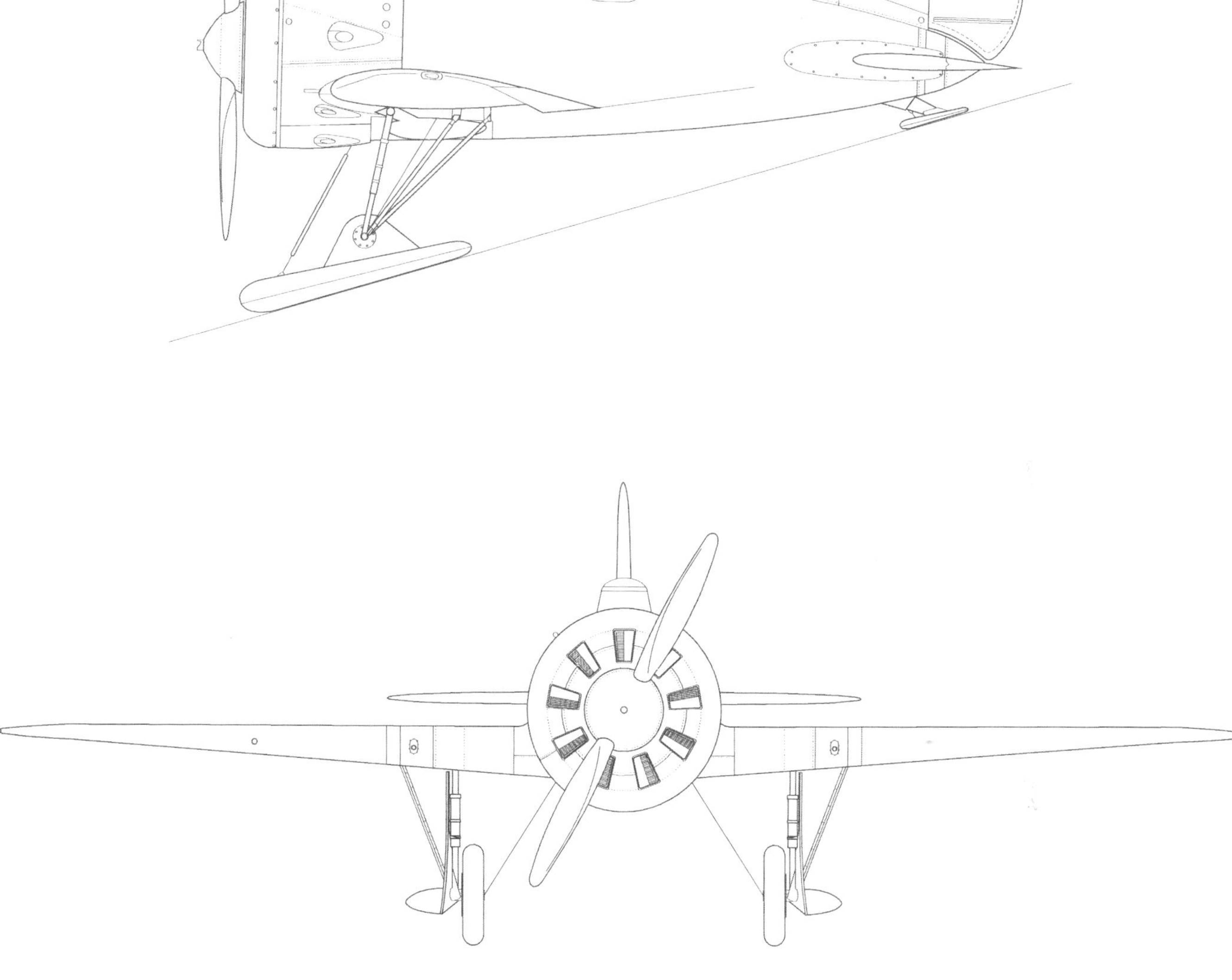

I-16 TYPE 5

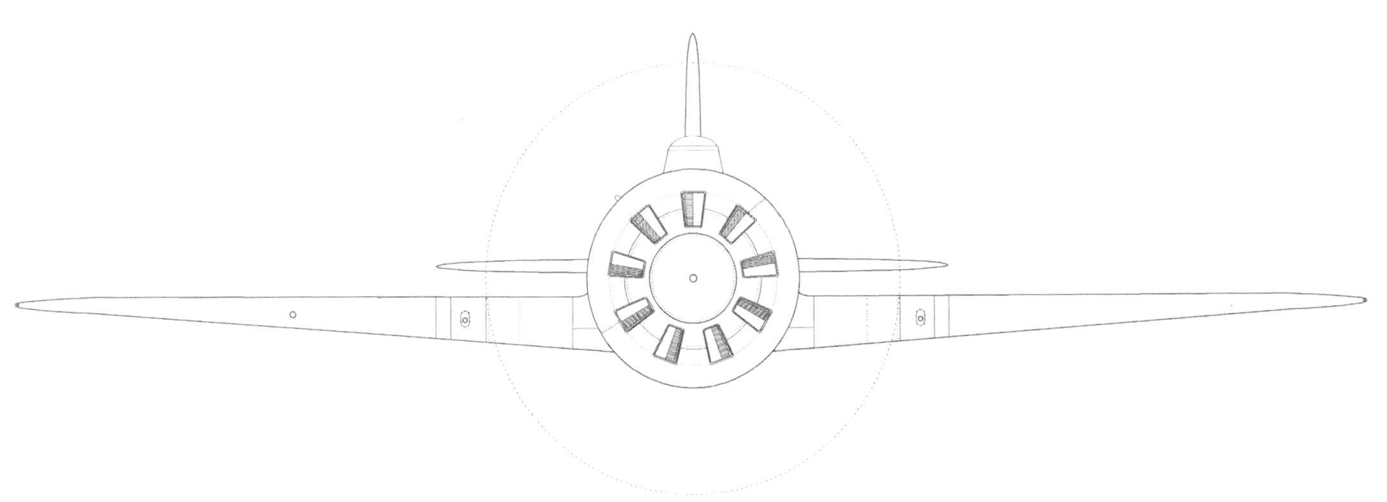

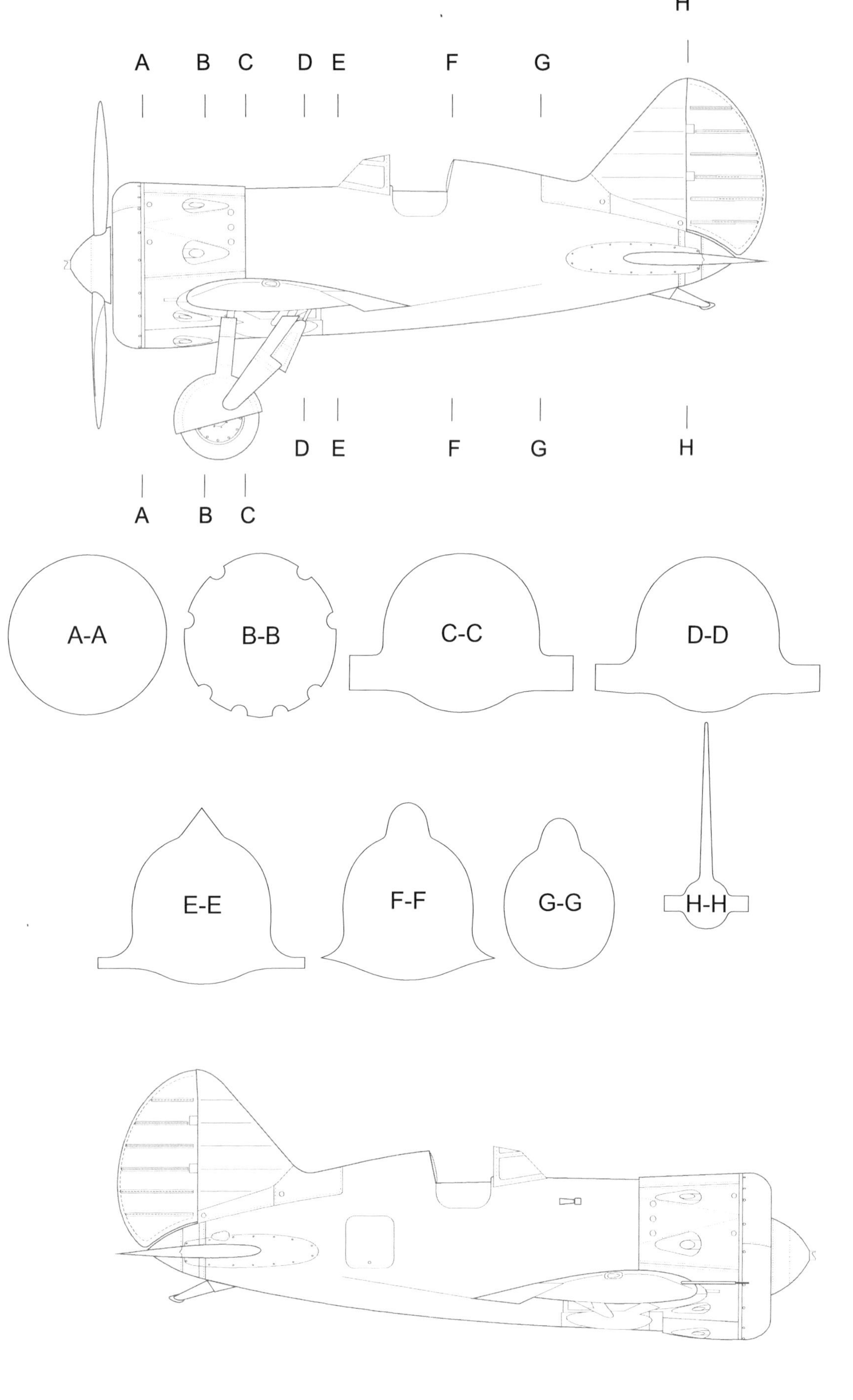

3

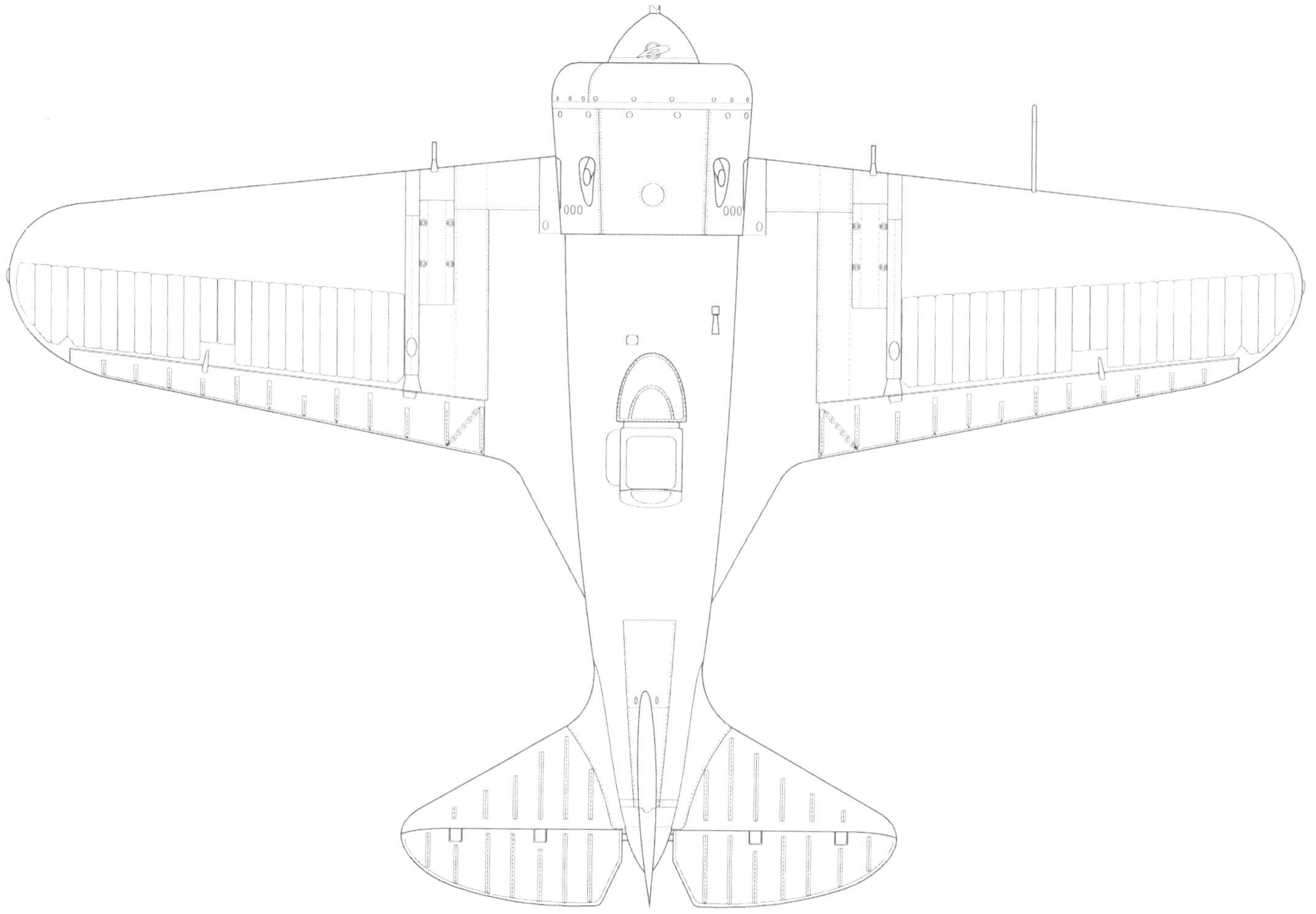

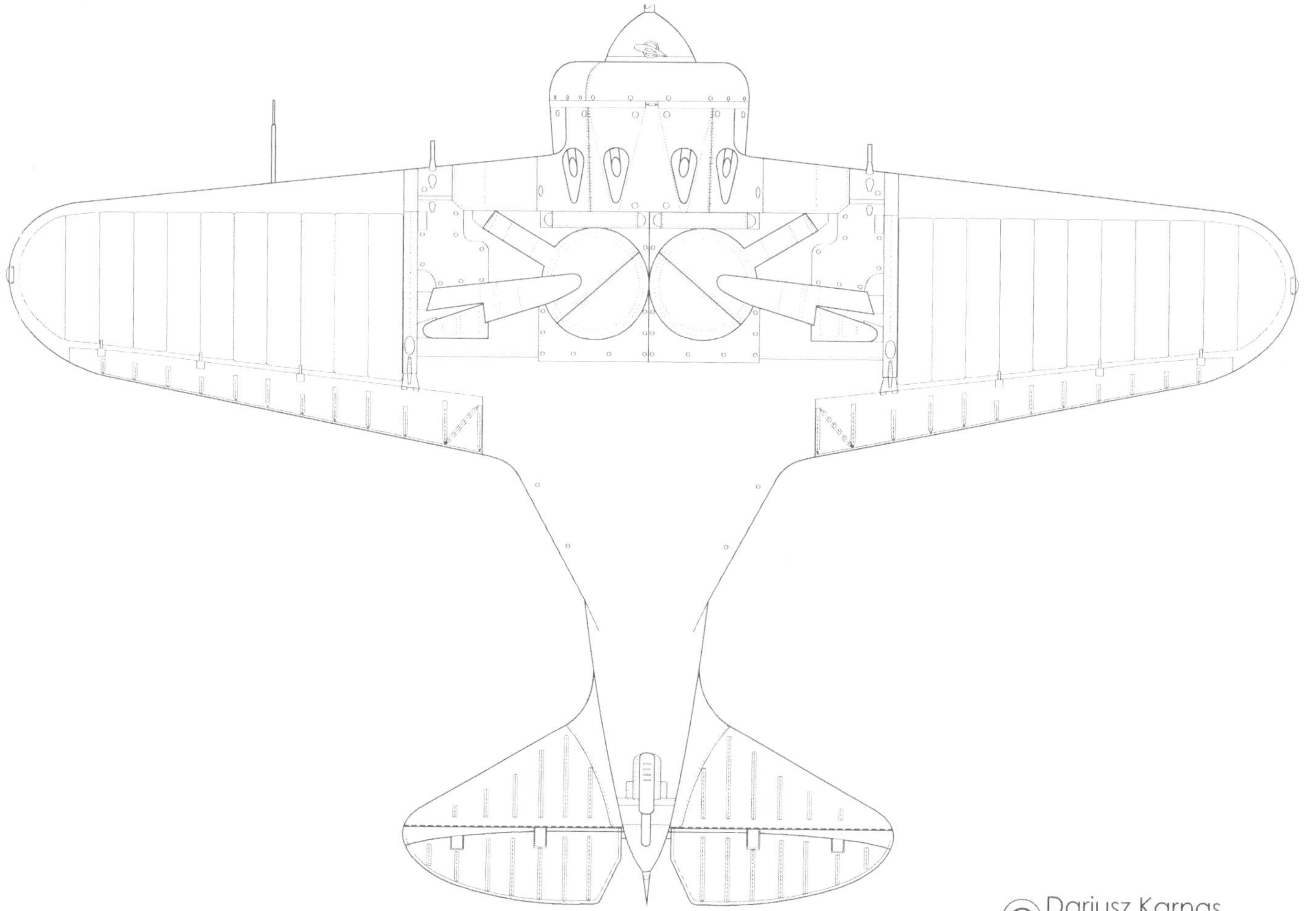

I-16 TYPE 5

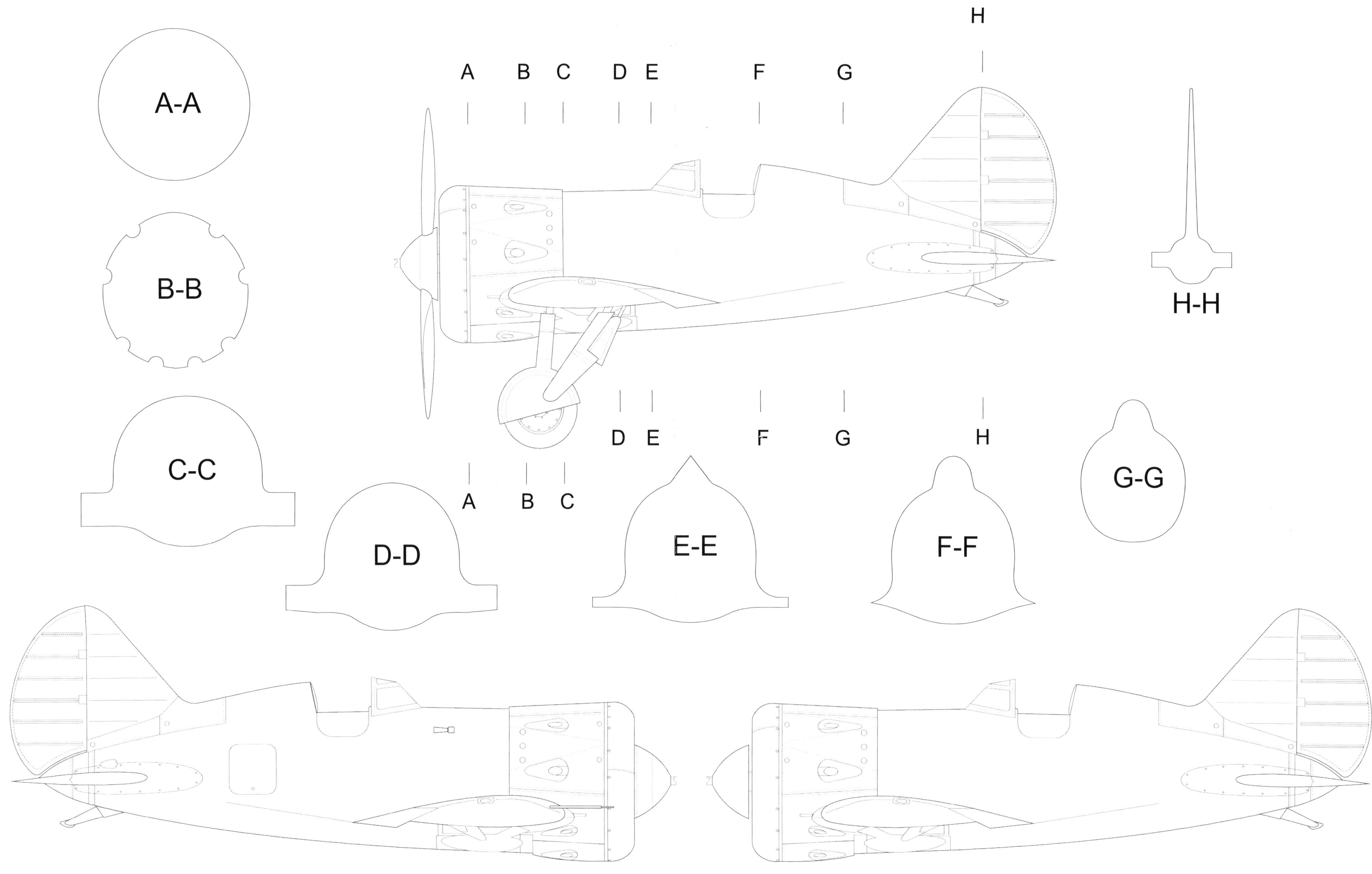

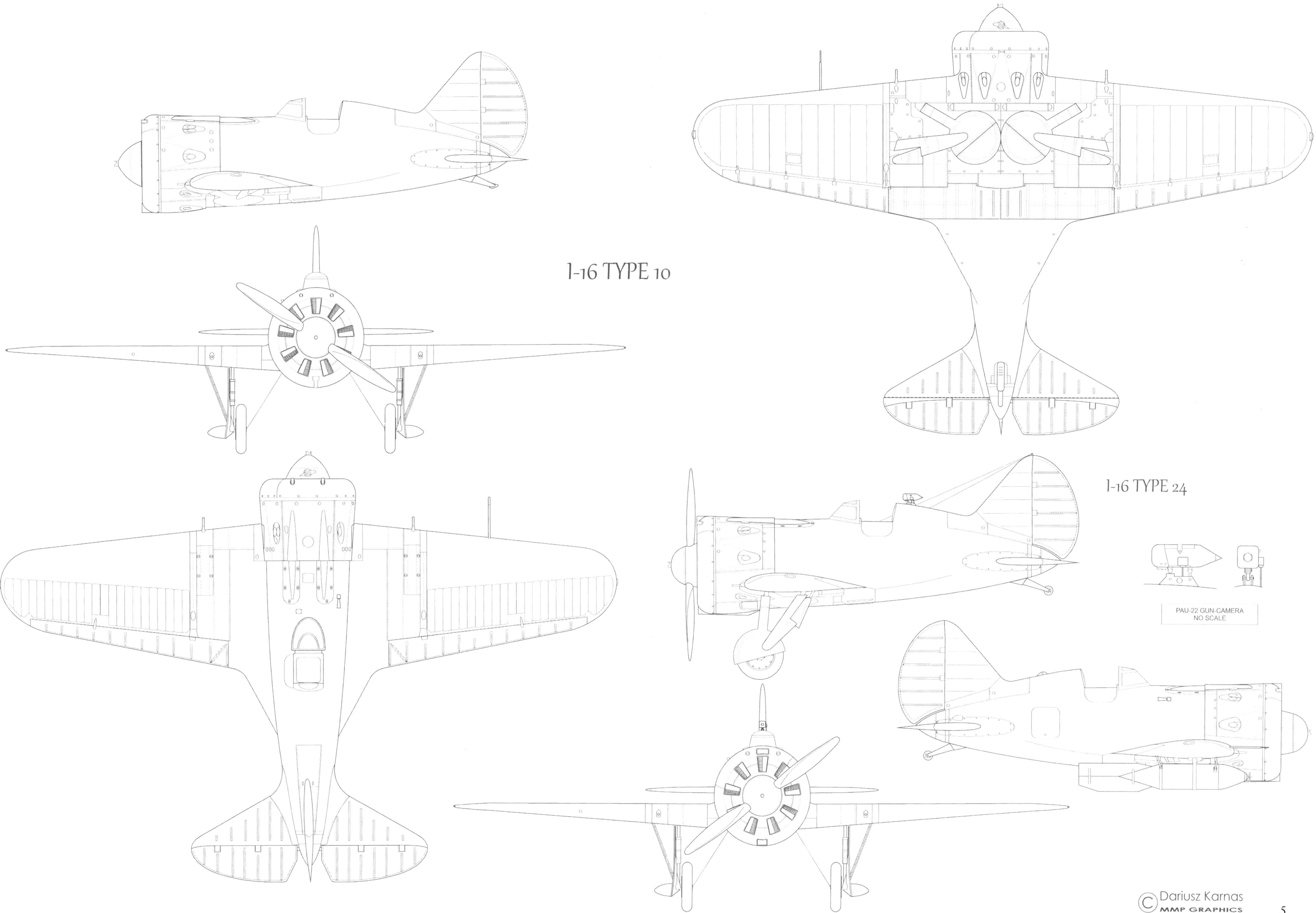
I-16 TYPE 10
I-16 TYPE 24
PAU-22 GUN-CAMERA
NO SCALE
Dariusz Karnas
MMP GRAPHICS

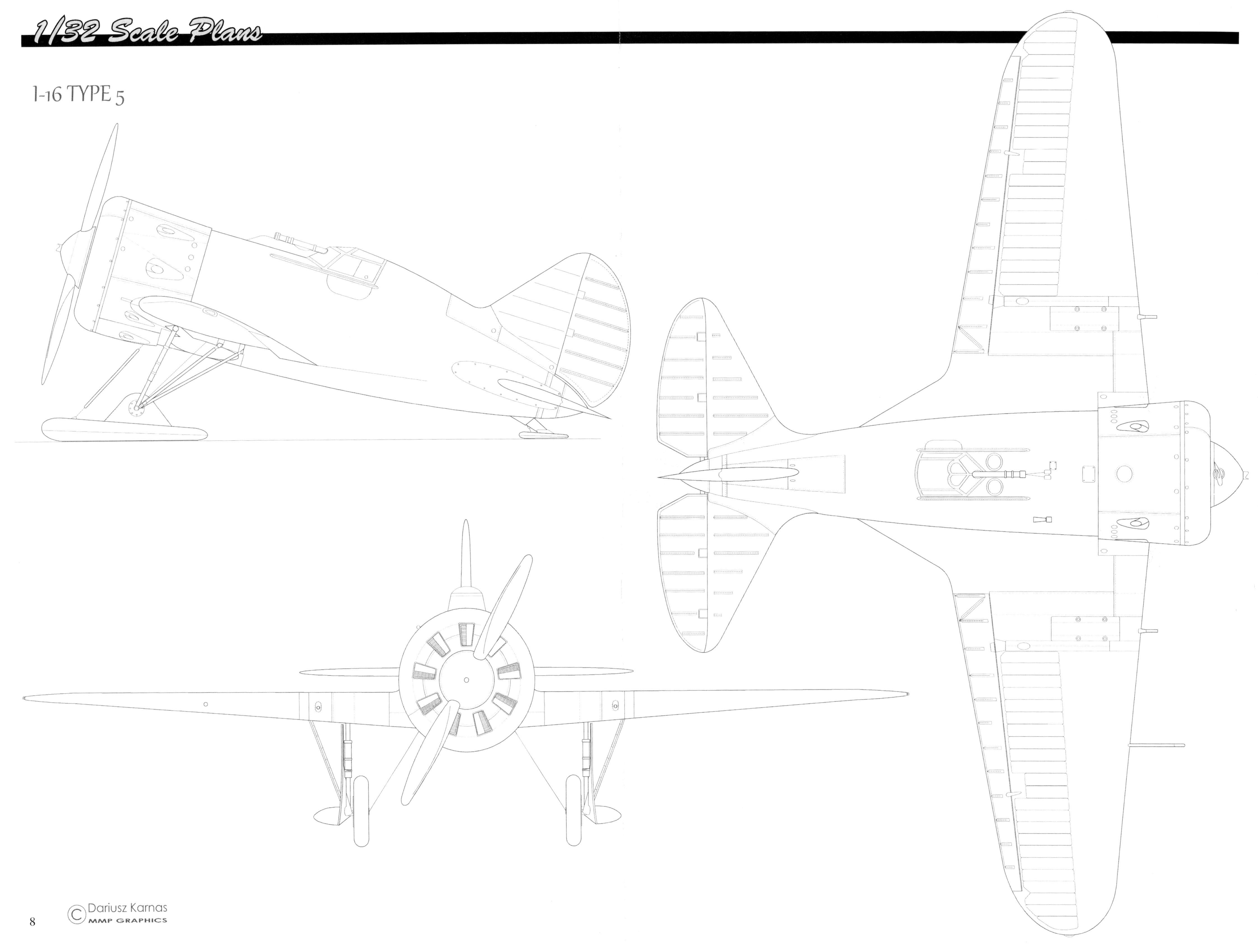

1/32 Scale Plans
I-16 TYPE 5
© Dariusz Karnas
MMP GRAPHICS
8

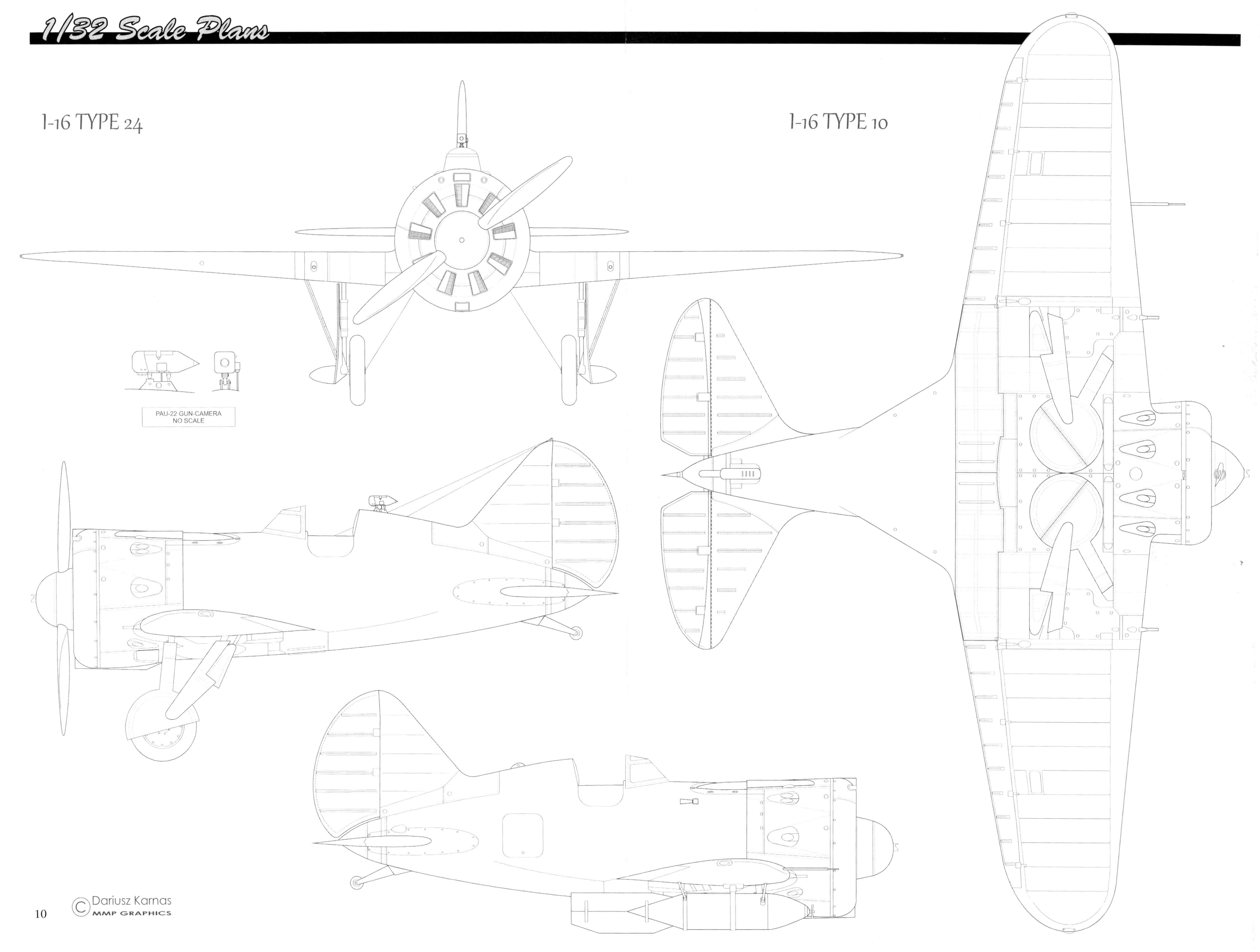

1/32 Scale Plans
I-16 TYPE 24
I-16 TYPE 10
PAU-22 GUN-CAMERA
NO SCALE
Dariusz Karnas
MMP GRAPHICS
10

I-16 TYPE 10

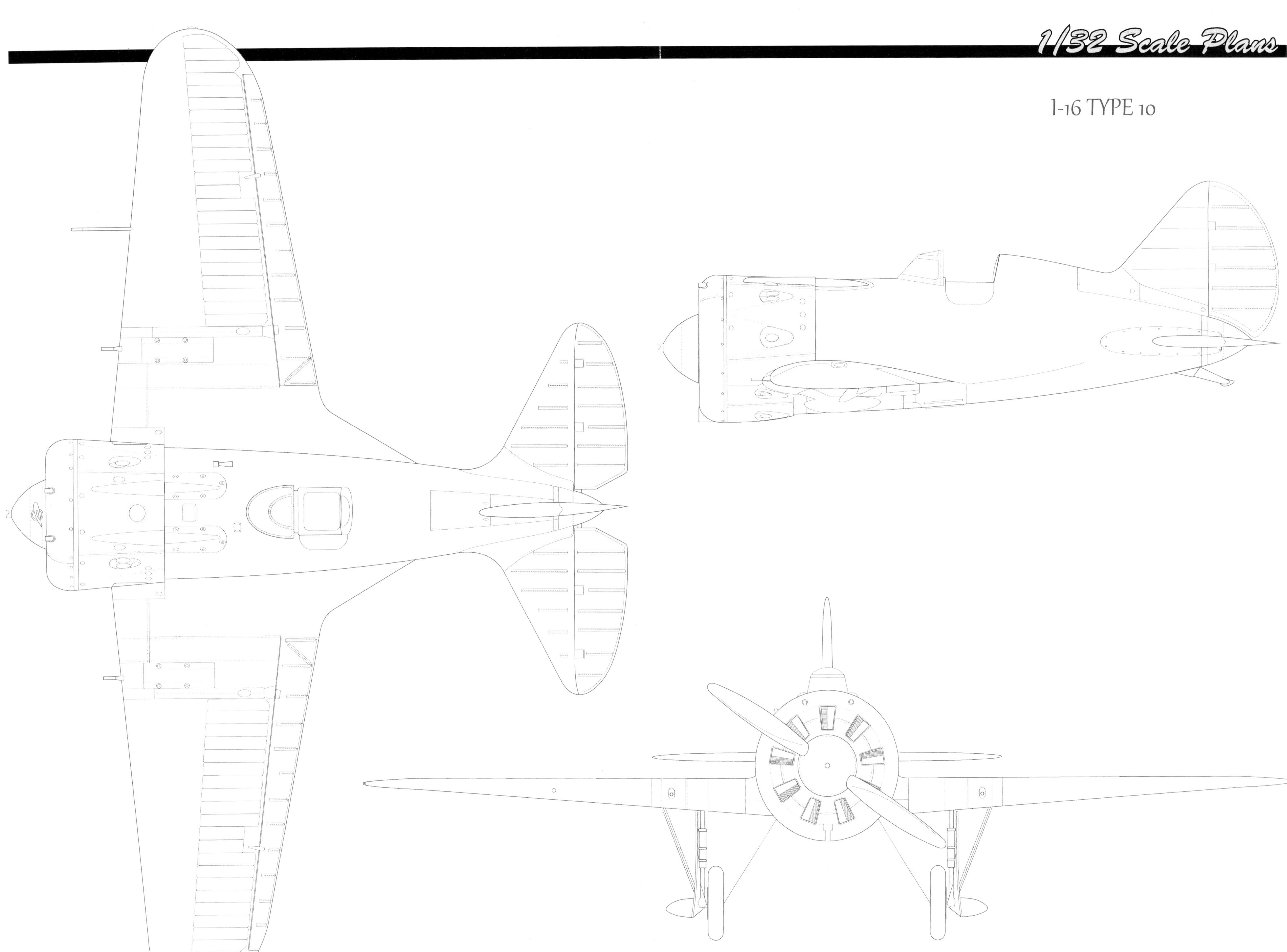